Have fun with the patterns.
Here are some ideas to try.

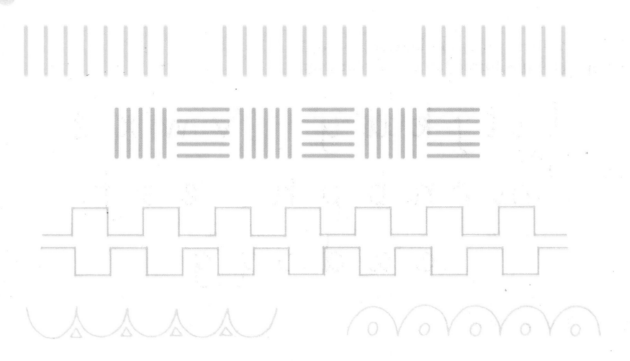

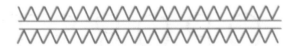

Try drawing the
patterns in different
sizes and colours.

Look at these groups of letters.
Each group is formed in a different way.

l i t j k u y   v w x z

m r n b p h   e s f

c a d o q g

Copy the letters.

Look at these capital letters.

A B C D E F G H I J K L M N
O P Q R S T U V W X Y Z

Copy the capital letters.

Now look at these numerals.

0 1 2 3 4 5 6 7 8 9

Copy the numerals.

Handwriting

Pupil Book 1

Look at these patterns.

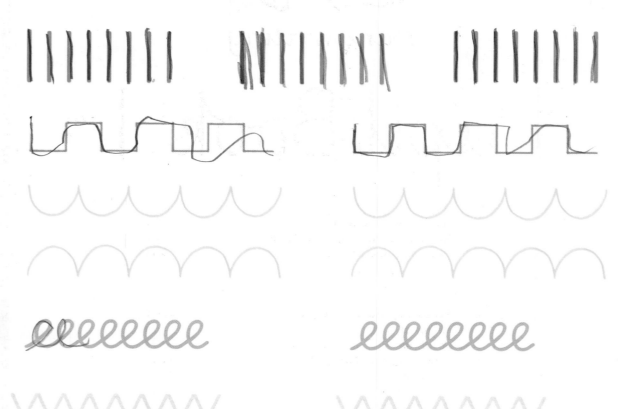

Copy the patterns.
They will help you with your handwriting.
Hold your pencil lightly.
Let the tip of your pencil flow over the paper.

Look at these groups of letters.

Ordinary letters

a c e i m n o p q r s

r s u v w x z

Letters with ascenders (tall letters)
These are much taller than ordinary letters.
t is not as tall as b, d, f, h, k and l.

b d f h k l t

Letters with descenders (letters with tails)
These are much deeper than ordinary letters.

g j p q y

Copy each group of letters.

Look at this example of joined writing.
What do you notice?

This sentence contains every letter of the alphabet.
Check it and see!

A quick brown fox

jumps over the lazy dog.

Look carefully at these words. They all contain the first join.

in name and

The first join is used when we join any letter in **Set 1** to any letter in **Set 2**.

Set 1
a c d e h i k l
m n s t u

→

Set 2
a c d e g i j
m n o p q r s
u v w x y

Copy this pattern.
It will help you with the first join.

Copy these pairs of letters.
Copy each line three times.

in   im   un   um

an   am   en   em

id   ig   ud   ug

Find the pairs of rhyming words.
Write them like this.

sun   bun

tin	him	man	jam
dim	hum	ham	can
sun	din	den	hem
mum	bun	gem	hen

Think of one more
rhyming word to
go with each pair.

Look at these words..
They all contain the first join.

sing and jump

Now copy the words above.

Make some words with *and*.

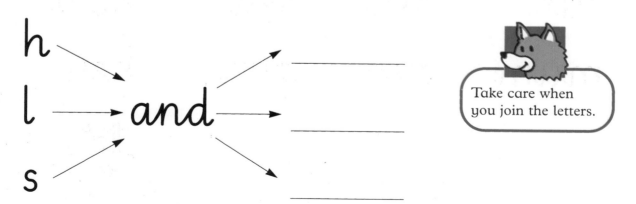

Take care when
you join the letters.

Write the *and* words.

● Now make some words with *end*.

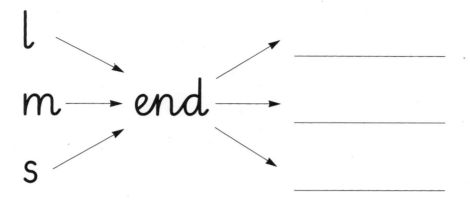

l
m → end →
s
_____
_____
_____

● Write the *end* words.

● Copy this sentence.

Lend a hand to the band.

● Copy these.

ing   ang   ung
sing   hang   lung

● Copy these.

imp   amp   ump
limp   damp   jump

Notice the shape of the letter e when it comes after a **Set 1** letter.

hid   hide

Now copy the words above.

Copy this pattern.
It will help you with e.

eeeeeeeeeee   eeeeeeeeeee

Add e to each word.
Write the pairs of words like this.

pin ——→ pine

can   dim   can

pal   mad   hid

din

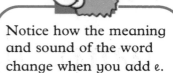

Notice how the meaning and sound of the word change when you add e.

10

When s comes after a **Set 1** letter,
it changes its shape.

smiles

Look carefully at the
two ways of writing s.
Notice the difference.

Write the word *smiles* three times.

as ds es is ks ls ms ts us

Copy the pairs of letters above.

one plate   lots of plates

Copy these words.

lane   lanes

date   dates

gate   gates

pine   pines

line   lines

Check that you have
written *e* and *s* correctly.

Look carefully at these words. They all contain the second join.
The join meets the ascender about halfway up.

tile chill bike

The second join is used when we join any letter in **Set 1** to any letter
in **Set 3**.

Set 1	Set 3
a c d e h i k l	b f h k l t
m n s t u	

Copy this pattern.
It will help you with the second join.

Write these words three times.

chilly

silly

Copy these pairs of letters.

ch ch ch ch ch

sh sh sh sh sh

th th th th th

Remember that the join meets the ascender about halfway up.

Choose ch, sh or th to complete each word.
Write the words.

___icken   ___eep   ___ief

___ink   ___imp   ___ell

Write three more words which begin with ch.
Do the same for sh and th.

13

Look at these words.
They all contain the second join.

skip slip stamp

Now copy the words above.

Copy these words.
They are all verbs.

A verb is a "doing" word.

skate skim skip skid
sleep slip slap slit
stack stick stamp stand

Now copy these.

a skinny skunk
a sleepy slug
a sticky stamp

Dot the i when you have
finished the word.

Cross the t when you
have finished the word.

14

Look at these words.
They all contain the second join.

pink silk tent

Each word in **Set A** rhymes with a word in **Set B**.
Find the rhyming words.
Write them like this.

silk ⟶ milk

Set A	
plant	tent
thank	pink
hulk	mint
silk	hunk

Set B	
think	lank
dent	milk
bunk	tint
chant	bulk

Look carefully at these words.
They all contain the third join.

toy want hard

The third join is used when we join any letter in **Set 4** to any letter in **Set 2**.

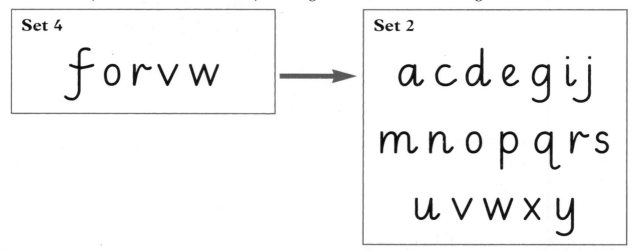

Set 4	Set 2
forvw	a c d e g i j m n o p q r s u v w x y

Copy these pairs of letters.

oa oa oa oa oa

Copy these words.

boat foal moan croak

coat goal loan soak

Copy these pairs of letters.

oo   oo   oo   oo   oo

Write the word that matches each picture.

moon *or* moan   crook *or* croak

fool *or* foal   boot *or* boat

Now write the four *oa* words.
Change the *oa* to *oo* in each word.
Write the words like this.

boat ⟶ boot

How are you getting on?
Look at the checklist.
Keep practising!

Look at this sentence.
All the words contain the third join.

Five fat frogs swam away
from five fierce fish.

Now copy the sentence above.

Copy the giant's words.

fe fi fo fum

Copy these words.

fish find fort
food fun fumble

Copy this tongue-twister.
There are a lot of *r* words in it.

Round and round the rugged rock the ragged rascal ran.

Copy these words.
Underline the places where the third join has been made.

<u>va</u>n vine
very verse
voice vixen
valley

want wish
write wall
water wind
window

ae When we join a **Set 1** letter to e, we use the first join.

we When we join a **Set 4** letter to e, we use the third join.

What difference can you see between the two ways of joining to e?

Copy these words.

fire hive wife give

life wire dive hive

knife live tire strife

Write these headings in your book.

ire words	ive words	ife words

Write each of the words in the box under the correct heading.

us   When we join a **Set 1** letter to s, we use the first join.

ws   When we join a **Set 4** letter to s, we use the third join.

What difference can you see between the two ways of joining to s?

Copy these patterns.

Copy these pairs of letters.

fs os rs vs ws

Add s to each of these words.
Write the new words three times.

piano   car   cow   roof

saw   chief   jar   banjo

Look carefully at these words.
They all contain the fourth join.
The join goes nearly to the top of the ascender.

smoke   girl   rob

The fourth join is used when we join any letter in **Set 4** to any letter in **Set 3**.

Set 4		Set 3
f o r v w	→	b f h k l t

Copy this word.

old   old   old   old

Copy these words three times.

cold told fold

hold gold

bold sold

22

Copy these pairs of letters.

wh wh wh wh

Copy this poem.
Notice all the *wh* words.

Remember that the join goes nearly to the top of the ascender.

Questions

Which and where
and why and when
Are words I keep saying
again and again.
Over and over
without any hitch –
When and where
and why and which.

by Peggy Noble

Look at these words.
They all contain the fourth join.

short dark curls

Now copy the words above.

Copy these patterns.
They will help you with the fourth join.

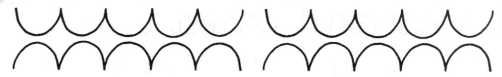

cork fork shorts sport

Copy these sentences.
Use one of the words in the box to fill each gap.

A bottle has a _____ .

Football is a _____ .

You eat with a _____ .

Sometimes I wear _____ .

Copy these.

irl irl irt irt

girl twirl dirt shirt

These sentences have got mixed up.
Write the sentences correctly.

very The hot.
girl was

Begin each sentence with
a capital letter and end it
with a full stop.

some on shirt.
He dirt got his

top twirl. I the
spinning made

How are you getting on?
Look at the checklist.
Keep practising!

The join between s and s can be difficult to make.
The join between f and f can be difficult too.
Look at this sentence.

"I will hiss and huff," said Billy Goat Gruff.

Now copy the sentence above.

Copy this pattern.
It will help you with the join.

Now copy these words.

Take special care
when the first s
comes after o.

passes blesses hisses

fusses bosses losses tosses

cliff puff stiff cuff stuff

The break letters

These are the eight break letters.
We never make a join after a break letter.

b g j p q x y z

○ Copy the break letters above.

○ Now copy these.

Leave a small space after each break letter.
Never join to or from z.

yellow yachts

queens on zebras

foxes in boxes

bugs on rugs

jumping jelly beans

We use commas (,) to separate words in a list.

Instead of a comma we put *and* between the last two things in the list.

cats, dogs, cows and hens

Copy these sentences. Put in the missing commas.

I have visited France Spain Greece and Italy.

In Technology I used a saw a drill a hammer and a knife.

My favourite subjects are Art Science and History.

We sometimes use commas when we write notes to people.

. Copy Sam's note to Father Christmas.

Notice how Sam uses commas.

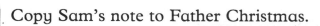

Dear Father Christmas,
    For Christmas I would really like some skates, a video game, a book on horses and some felt-tips. I hope I will be lucky.
        Thank you,
        Sam

Write a note like this to Father Christmas or to your parents.
List at least four things which you would like for Christmas or your birthday.

Look at these numerals and number words.

1 2 3 4 5 6 7 8 9 10

one two three four five
six seven eight nine ten

Copy each numeral and each number word three times.

Now write all the numerals from 1 to 30 as quickly as you can.
Time yourself.
Repeat the experiment.
Try to improve on your speed.

Copy these number words and write the numerals which go with them.

eleven thirty seventeen
twenty fifteen nineteen
twenty-eight twelve

Read this chart.

Name of animal	Length	Weight
fox	120 cm	10 kg
grey squirrel	30 cm	1 kg
rabbit	45 cm	2 kg
hare	70 cm	6 kg
fallow deer	170 cm	90 kg

Write a sentence about each animal.

Which animal is longest?
Which animal is shortest?
Which animal is heaviest?
Which animal is lightest?

Answer the questions in complete sentences.

three mice steal cheese

Make a chart like this in your book.

Find the *ee* words.
Copy them into the chart.

Find the *ea* words.
Copy them into the chart.

ee	*ea*

cheek   cheap   deep   deal

eat   free   see   east

feet   seek   peach   speed

read   seat   speak   three

steal   cheese   heal   creep

Copy the sentences.
Fill each gap with *ee* or *ea*.

Thr_e_ sh_e_p were lost on the b_ea_ch.

The br_ee_ze blew a l_e_f down.

The qu_ee_n fell asl_ee_p.

Sw_ee_p the str_ea_t cl_ea_n.

How are you getting on?
Look at the checklist.
Keep practising!

fast   slow

 Choose the correct word from each pair.
Write the sentences.

short long

The lorry is _____.

big small

Ar elephant is _____.

soft hard

Candy floss is _____.

 A lemon is <u>sour</u> but chocolate is <u>sweet</u>.

 A hippo is fat but a snake is thin.

 Ice is cold but fire is hot.

 Ben got wet but Sam stayed dry.

 Try not to write too slowly or too quickly.

Make a list like this.

Things an astronaut needs
spacesuit
helmet

Look at these words.
Eight of them are things you would need if you were an astronaut.
Write these words on your list.

maps   helmet   bicycle   food

flippers   torch   radio   boots

hamster   spacesuit   oxygen

Here are some things that make people happy.

 stroking a cat

learning to swim

 a fizzy drink

a sunny morning

 finishing a puzzle

Write them as a list poem like this.

Happiness is stroking a cat.
Happiness is...

Add two more things that make **you** happy.

Make sure your writing does not slope in different directions.

spring   summer   autumn   winter

Look at these pictures of what the giant had for dinner.

Now write these sentences in the correct order.

Next he ate some chestnut trees.

Last of all he drank the sea.

Then he ate a house near me.

First he ate a hive of bees.

by Ian McMillan

These instructions for having a bath have got mixed up.
Write the sentences in the correct order.

Try to leave the same amount of space between words.

Step into the bath.

Step out of the bath.

Wash yourself all over.

Take off your clothes.

Put the plug in the bath.

Fill the bath with warm water.

Dry yourself with a towel.

When we write a question, we put a question mark at the end.

How old are you?

I am 100 years old.

? ? ? ? ? ? ? ? ? ? ? ? ? ?

Copy these question marks.

Copy these questions. Write the answers.

How old are you?

What is the weather like?

When must you write a question mark?

How did you get to school?

40

These questions and answers have got muddled up.
Write each question with the correct answer.

What noise does a dog make? A dog quacks.

What noise does a lion make? A lion hisses.

What noise does a mouse make? A mouse barks.

What noise does a duck make? A duck roars.

What noise does a snake make? A snake squeaks.

I am a <u>dentist</u>.

I look after your teeth.

These words tell us about people's jobs.

optician mechanic plumber

Use one of the words above to fill each of the gaps.

I am a _____.

I mend water pipes.

I am a _____.

I mend cars.

I am an _____.

I check your eyes.

bakery reservoir
aviary cinema hive

Copy the sentences.
Fill each gap with one of the words in the box.

Films are shown in a _____.

Bees are kept in a _____.

Water is stored in a _____.

Bread is made in a _____.

Birds are kept in an _____.

In an acrostic poem, the title is hidden in the poem in a special way.

It is important to write neatly and clearly so that other people can read what you have written.

Blackbird
In the sky,
Right up in the clouds,
Dancing on the wind.

Look at this poem and the poem on page 45.
Can you find the titles?

Copy these two acrostic poems.

Happy days
Out playing with friends,
Lots of fun
In the garden,
Doing whatever I like,
Away from school,
Yellow buttercups,
Sun, sea and sand.

Make up an acrostic poem of your own.

Sometimes people have to write very accurate descriptions.

Wanted

Name: **Bill Benbow**

Age: **38 years**

Height: **1 m 85 cm**

Hair: **Fair, curly**

Eyes: **Brown (wears glasses)**

Special features: **Scar on right cheek**

Last seen wearing: **Jeans, check shirt**

Use the information above to write a description of Bill Benbow.
Write in complete sentences.

When Mrs. Smith got home from work one day, someone had broken into her shed.

shed

gate

door

path

broken fence

bushes

muddy footprints

Mrs. Smith went to the police station.
She was asked to write a description of what she had seen.
Pretend you are Mrs. Smith.
Write a description for the police.

How well have you done?
Look at the checklist.

Copy these patterns carefully.

∪∪∪∪∪ eeeeeee

ccccccc oooooo

You have come to the end of Pupil Book 1. This is a good time to check your writing.

Copy these words in your best handwriting.

him sun mends lamp

chill thinks shelf elephant

croaks write wife cows

where smoke girl stiff

Copy this sentence in your best handwriting.

A quick brown fox jumps over the lazy dog.